ENIGMAS *of* HISTORY

THE MYSTERIES OF
THE MAYA

WORLD BOOK

a Scott Fetzer company
Chicago
www.worldbook.com

World Book edition of "Enigmas de la historia" by Editorial Sol 90.

Enigmas de la historia
El ocaso de los Mayas

This edition licensed from Editorial Sol 90 S.L.
Copyright 2013 Editorial Sol S.L. All rights reserved.

English-language revised edition copyright 2014
World Book, Inc.
Enigmas of History
The Mysteries of the Maya

World Book, Inc.
233 North Michigan Avenue
Suite 2000
Chicago, Illinois, 60601 U.S.A.

For information about other World Book publications,
visit our website at **www.worldbook.com** or call
1-800-967-5325.

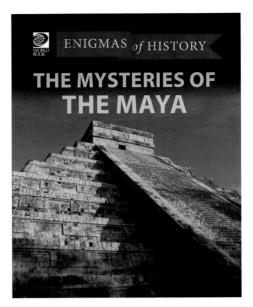

The pyramid El Castillo, also known as the Temple of
Kukulkan, dominates the site of Chichén Itzá, once a
powerful Mayan city from around A.D. 900 to about
A.D. 1200, in what is now Mexico. Kukulkan was a
god represented as a feathered snake. When the
pyramid was in use, priests climbed the stairs and
held ceremonies in the temple at the top.

© Danny Lehman, Corbis Images

Library of Congress Cataloging-in-Publication Data

Ocaso de los Mayas. English.
   The mysteries of the Maya. -- English-language revised
edition.
      pages cm. -- (Enigmas of history)
   Includes index.
   Summary: "An exploration of the questions and mysteries
that have puzzled scholars and experts about the Ancient
Maya culture. Features include a timeline, map, fact boxes,
biographies of famous experts on Maya culture, places to see
and visit, a glossary, further readings, and index"-- Provided
by publisher.
   ISBN 978-0-7166-2663-3
   1. Mayas--History--Juvenile literature. 2. Mayas--Social life
and customs--Juvenile literature. I. World Book, Inc.
F1435.M96 2014
972.81--dc23
                              2014004729

Set ISBN: 978-0-7166-2660-2

Printed in China by PrintWORKS Global Services,
Shenzhen, Guangdong
1st printing May 2014

Staff

Executive Committee

President
Donald D. Keller

Vice President and Editor in Chief
Paul A. Kobasa

Vice President, Sales
Sean Lockwood

Vice President, Finance
Anthony Doyle

Director, Marketing
Nicholas A. Fryer

Director, Human Resources
Bev Ecker

Editorial

*Associate Director,
Annuals and Topical Reference*
Scott Thomas

*Managing Editor,
Annuals and Topical Reference*
Barbara A. Mayes

*Senior Editor,
Annuals and Topical Reference*
Christine Sullivan

Manager, Indexing Services
David Pofelski

Administrative Assistant
Ethel Matthews

*Manager, Contracts & Compliance
(Rights & Permissions)*
Loranne K. Shields

*Editorial Administration
Director, Systems and Projects*
Tony Tills

*Senior Manager, Publishing
Operations*
Timothy Falk

Manufacturing/Production

Director
Carma Fazio

Manufacturing Manager
Barbara Podczerwinski

*Production/Technology
Manager*
Anne Fritzinger

Proofreader
Nathalie Strassheim

Graphics and Design

Art Director
Tom Evans

Senior Designer
Don Di Sante

Media Researcher
Jeff Heimsath

*Manager, Cartographic
Services*
Wayne K. Pichler

Senior Cartographer
John M. Rejba

Marketing

Marketing Manager
Tamika Robinson

Marketing Specialist
Annie Suhy

Contents

TIKAL'S GREAT PLAZA
Pyramids built during the
Classic Period rise above the
rain forest in the ancient city
of Tikal, now a national park in
Guatemala.

The Magnificent Maya

The ancient Maya have been slow to reveal their secrets, despite the best efforts of archaeologists and scholars over the past 150 years. Excavations of their ruined cities and treasure-filled tombs have uncovered impressive architecture and glorious art. Studies of their remarkable writing system have revealed much about Maya history, religion, and scientific achievements. Yet mysteries remain. Where did the Maya come from? Why did they abandon some of their greatest cities beginning in the A.D. 800's, at the height of their civilization? Why did their writing remain so mysterious for so long? What happened to their books? What did they know about the movement of the sun and planets?

The ancient Maya were never united under a single government. Nor did they ever have an empire, like those of the Aztecs and other Mesoamerican cultures. The Maya civilization actually included some 28 ethnic groups. But because they spoke related versions of a language and shared religious beliefs, scholars consider these groups as part of one culture. The homeland of the ancient Maya stretched across the rain forests of modern-day Belize and northern Guatemala; the mountainous highlands of what are now southern Mexico, southern Guatemala, northwestern El Salvador, and northwestern Honduras; and the plains of what is now southern Mexico, particularly the Yucatán Peninsula.

Scholars organize the history of the ancient Maya into three periods. The Preclassic Period began about 1800 B.C. and ended about A.D. 250. The Classic Period began around A.D. 250 and ended around 900. The Postclassic Period began around 900 and lasted through the 1500's, as the Maya were gradually overcome by Spanish conquerors.

The Classic Period marked the peak of Maya civilization. During this period, the Maya founded their greatest cities and made remarkable achievements in the arts and sciences. The cities were dominated by large, impressive buildings that included pyramids and temples set atop tall mounds. In these structures, archaeologists have found tombs filled with jade jewelry, beautifully painted ceramic vessels, and statues carved from rock. Maya cities also had buildings for government officials, multiroom houses, markets, ball courts, and plazas. During the Classic Period, the Maya perfected the art of building monuments called stelae. These large stone slabs were carved to record dates and significant events or ceremonies in the lives of the Maya rulers and their families.

The ancient Maya also made great advances in astronomy and mathematics. The sun was the center of Maya life and religion, and the priests measured the solar cycle with great precision. They also calculated the cycles of the moon and stars. They made tables predicting eclipses and describing the orbit of the planet Venus. The Maya became the first people in ancient America to use a symbol for the idea of zero—an idea unknown to Europeans until the 1400's.

Maya priests used astronomy and mathematics to develop a complex dating system that included three calendars, which served as the basis of their religious life.

The calendars began on August 13, 3114 B.C., the date on which the Maya believed the latest cycle had begun. The Maya believed that history occurred in an endless, repeating cycle. Priests recorded events at all times to try to learn what the future would bring.

The Maya were also skilled farmers. Using an efficient system of terraces and raised beds, they were able to produce an abundance of food from relatively poor soils.

Despite advances in deciphering ancient Maya writing, scholars still have much to read and understand to learn about the Maya's religion, political relations, society, and art. There are also hundreds of Maya sites to discover and excavate. Fortunately, archaeologists and scholars have another great resource in their exploration of the ancient Maya. The Maya never disappeared. Groups of Maya live today in the Yucatán, Belize, and Honduras. Descendants of those who survived the Spanish conquest, they have challenged history by preserving their languages, many aspects of their religion, and many of their ancient traditions.

TIKAL'S TEMPLE OF THE GREAT JAGUAR tops a pyramid that contains the tomb of Jasaw Chan K'awiil I, one of the city's greatest rulers.

Who Were the Ancient Maya?

Archaeologists and other scholars continue to discover exciting new information about the world of the Maya.

The Maya created one of the greatest civilizations in Mesoamerica in the centuries before the arrival of European explorers in the early 1500's. The ancient Maya never lived in a united empire. Political regions formed and broke up based on alliances and rivalries between city-states. Instead, Maya civilization arose from numerous groups that spoke related languages and shared common religious beliefs.

The stage for the splendor and decline of the ancient Maya was an area spanning almost 120,000 square miles (310,000 square kilometers) in the modern Mexican states of Yucatán, Tabasco, Chiapas, and Quintana Roo. The ancient Maya homeland also included the plateau and low

lands of what are now northern Guatemala and parts of Belize, El Salvador, and Honduras.

BEGINNINGS

The earliest evidence for the ancestors of the Maya dates back some 10,000 years. These ancestors lived by hunting wild animals and gathering plants that grew naturally in their environment. By about 1800 B.C., the early Maya had begun living in small villages. They raised crops and gathered food from the surrounding forest. By about 800 B.C., some Maya villages had grown into cities. The first large Maya pyramids were built from 600 to 400 B.C.

ACHIEVEMENTS

Some Maya achievements rivaled those of ancient Egypt

and Classical Greece and Rome. Maya pyramids rank among the greatest in the Americas. Maya paintings show a high level of artistic expression. Their writing, as well as their calendars, are considered the most advanced in the ancient Americas.

The Maya were an agricultural people who were among the first to cultivate corn. They worshiped many gods related to the cultivation of the earth. Their farming techniques were sometimes ingenious. They practiced *slash-and-burn agriculture* (a system where vegetation is burnt and used as fertilizer for otherwise infertile land) in the forests. In other regions, they created terraces and raised beds for their crops. They understood that crops should be rotated to let the soil recover. These methods helped Maya farmers grew enough food for large populations of city dwellers.

LEADERS AND FOLLOWERS

Maya society was divided into two main classes. The supreme ruler of a city was also the chief priest. The founder of the ruler's family was considered a god and the source of the ruler's authority. The chief and his extended family lived in ceremonial centers. In contrast, the *peasants* (farmers and laborers) lived in huts spread through nearby forests and around farm fields.

Scholars believe the Maya began to establish political units in the form of cities around 800 B.C., at the end of the Preclassic Period. This political process occurred in different stages in such different places as El Mirador, Tikal, and Calakmul.

During the Classic Period, the center of Maya civilization was the Petén region, now part of Guatemala. Various city-states flourished there, including Tikal, one of the largest and most populated.

The Maya soon developed a writing system based on *glyphs* (symbols). The glyphs were carved on *stelae* (sculp-

tured stone slabs) and other stone monuments. The Maya also wrote on paper made of fig bark that was folded into books called *codices*.

In the 1960's, *epigraphers* (scholars who study inscriptions) made great advances in decoding Maya glyphs. As a result, they were able to precisely date a number of historic events.

CONFLICT BETWEEN CITY-STATES

War was an important part of Maya society. Maya city-states fought one another for land, natural resources, and workers. Some Maya rulers attacked other city-states to prove how powerful they were.

A stela found in Tikal revealed that a high-ranking military officer named Siyah K'ak', also known as "Fire Is Born," conquered Tikal on January 16 in A.D. 378. Siyah K'ak' appears to have been a lieutenant of the ruler of the rival city of Teotihuacan. From then until the 600's, Teotihuacan exerted a considerable influence over the Maya and other groups in southern Mexico.

In the 600's, Tikal became a superpower by conquering or making alliances with other city-states. But Tikal also attracted enemies.

Over time, the city-state of Calakmul, in the Mexican lowlands of the modern state of Campeche, became Tikal's main rival. The clash between the two city-states divided the Maya and helped end five centuries of splendor.

DECLINE

During the Postclassic Period of Maya history, the population shrank quickly. The Maya no longer wrote on stelae, and they abandoned their monumental buildings and even some

cities in the lowlands. Why? Archaeologists and scholars are not certain. The Maya may have exhausted their natural resources or suffered natural catastrophes or internal uprisings.

After the fall of the southern cities, the Maya civilization continued its decline in the Yucatán Peninsula. Two neighboring kingdoms developed there under the influence of a foreign people known as the Toltecs. The Toltecs spread the worship of Quetzalcoatl, the Feathered Serpent.

The first kingdom, Chichén Itzá, flourished as a commercial and religious center beginning around A.D. 1000. Around 1200, the city was suddenly abandoned, possibly because it was defeated in battle. The second kingdom was Mayapan. It fell in the mid-1400's.

SPANISH CONQUEST

When the Spaniards arrived in the Yucatán, the Maya were already in decline. The Spanish conquest lasted for 19 years, from 1527 to 1546. The Maya in what is now modern-day Guatemala were almost completely conquered by 1530. The forces of Spanish leader Pedro de Alvarado conquered the Quiché with the support of the rival Kakchiquel people. Both groups were of Maya origin. The last stronghold of Maya resistance was not subdued until 1697. Located in the Guatemalan region of El Petén, the stronghold was led by the Itzá, who previously had their capital in Chichén Itzá.

A STORY IN WOOD

A king (center in image) rides on a *palanquin* (litter with curtains) during a military celebration, in an elaborate carving from a temple in Tikal.

UNCOVERING A CITY

Workers labor to remove jungle vegetation covering the ruins of the main temple in the ancient city of Tulum in a lithograph by English architect Frederick Catherwood. Catherwood and American diplomat John Lloyd Stephens were among the first to study ancient Maya sites.

Sacrifices in the Cenotes

To please their gods, the Maya commonly sacrificed animals and practiced *bloodletting* (drawing blood from the fingertips, earlobes, and other parts of the body with a sharp object). Human sacrifices took place but occurred much less often than they did among neighboring civilizations, particularly the Aztecs.

Many Maya remains have been found in *cenotes* (sink holes or pits) in the Yucatán Peninsula. Until about 1960, most scholars believed that the Maya used the cenotes of this region only for human sacrifice. Specifically, they believed that many virgins had been thrown into the cenotes. This belief led to the theory that for the Maya, the cenotes represented fertility. The holes may also have been a symbolic link with the underworld, inhabited by the dead. The Maya called this underworld Xibalba and believed it had a relationship with the night.

Studies carried out by such experts as Mexican archaeologist Guillermo de Anda argued against this theory, however. In his explorations of cenotes in Chichén Itzá, de Anda found mostly the remains of children (around 10 years old) and adult males.

The cenotes may have been used for reasons other than human sacrifice, other archaeologists have concluded. Evidence suggests that the bodies of children who had died of natural causes were sometimes removed from their graves. After the flesh was removed from their bodies, their remains were thrown into the cenotes to re-enact the Maya myth of the Hero Twins. In this myth, two brothers are transformed into the sun and the moon.

SACRED CENOTES
One of the two cenotes in Chichén Itzá was used for rituals (above), while another provided fresh water for the people of the city.

Secret Ceremony

Mexican archaeologist Guillermo de Anda contends that during the Maya ceremony in honor of the rain god Chac Xib Chaac, the cries of the children who were going to be sacrificed were thought to resemble the croaking of frogs. During the ceremony, priests cut apart the bodies of the victims and removed the victims' hearts. The remains were then thrown into a sacred cenote.

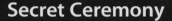

GOD OF FERTILITY
The king of Copán is shown on an incense burner with froglike features linked to the rain god Chac.

LEARNING ABOUT THE ANCIENT MAYA
In 1839, the world outside Central America first heard of the ancient Maya thanks to United States diplomat John Lloyd Stephens. An explorer and travel writer, he also traveled to Egypt, Arabia, Israel, Greece, Turkey, Russia, and Poland. Stephens's interest in the Maya started in 1834 when he read a report about the Copán ruins (in modern Honduras) written by a Central

American military officer. The report included many maps and drawings that caught Stephens's attention. Stephens soon undertook a journey to the Maya homeland, where he saw the ruins of the cities of Palenque, Labna, Kabah, Uxmal, Chichén Itzá, and Tulum. He also saw Copán, which he bought for $50.

Stephens described his adventures in two books: *Incidents of Travel in Central America, Chiapas, and Yucatan* (1841) and *Incidents of Travel in Yucatan* (1843). The reports included beautiful drawings of the monumental ruins set against the jungle landscape by English architect Frederick Catherwood, Stephens's traveling companion.

ARCHAEOLOGICAL EXPLORATION

In the 1880's, archaeologists began to explore Maya sites. From 1881 to 1894, the Englishman Alfred Percival Maudslay carried out seven expeditions to the Maya homeland. Maudslay made photographs and drawings and wrote descriptions of the buildings and monuments he saw. He also made plaster casts of reliefs and inscriptions and took home priceless objects. Many of these objects now belong to the British Museum in London. Maudslay was the first to take photographs and draw a map of Tikal.

KINGS IN STONE

Carvings representing 4 of Copán's 16 rulers during the Classic Period cover one side of a sculpture called the Q Altar. The remaining rulers appear on the three other sides of the altar.

A Maya Timeline

The Maya have one of the longest histories in Mesoamerica. Over thousands of years, they established villages and cities. They also maintained wide contacts—not always peaceful—with other peoples in the region.

Many People, One Culture

The Maya arose more than 3,000 years ago in what is now central Guatemala. They spread throughout much of southern Mexico and Central America. Although some groups of Maya developed different traditions, they remained united as a culture because of their common religious beliefs and related languages. Today, more than 7 million Maya descendants live in Belize, El Salvador, Guatemala, Honduras, and Mexico.

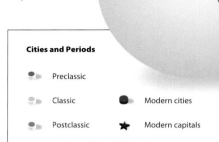

Maya Culture

PYRAMIDS

In their cities, the Maya built tall pyramids of limestone with small temples on top. Priests climbed the steep stairs of the pyramids to perform ceremonies in the temples. Maya leaders were sometimes buried within the pyramids. The Maya's largest-known pyramids have been found in the ancient city of El Mirador and date from the Postclassic Period. La Danta, in what is now Guatemala, is the tallest pyramid in the Americas.

Cities and Periods

- Preclassic
- Classic   ● Modern cities
- Postclassic   ★ Modern capitals

Chiapa de Corz

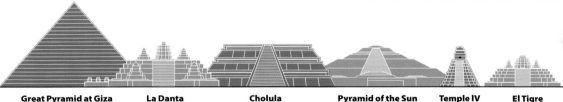

Great Pyramid at Giza	La Danta	Cholula	Pyramid of the Sun	Temple IV	El Tigre
Egypt	Guatamala	Mexico	Mexico	Guatamala	Guatamala
450 ft (140 m)	236 ft (78 m)	216 ft (66 m)	234 ft (71 m)	210 ft (64 m)	180 ft (55 m)

Periods in Maya History

Scholars organize the history of the ancient Maya into three periods: the Preclassic (the appearance of the early Maya); the Classic (the peak of Maya civilization); and the Postclassic (the decline of Maya power).

11,000 B.C.
The first groups of nomads and hunters appear in the Yucatán in modern-day Mexico and the modern-day *department* (state) of El Petén in Guatemala. They begin to establish small groups of settlements.

circa 2000 B.C.
The Maya civilization arises in the lowlands of what is now Guatemala. The Maya may have adopted writing, numbers, and pyramids from the Olmec, who lived west of the Maya.

100 B.C.
The city of Teotihuacan begins to influence the religious, cultural, and commercial life of the Maya.

Year A.D. 1

250

3114 - 3113 B.C.
The world was created during these two years, according to Maya calendars.

400 B.C.
The Maya use the first known solar calendars made of stone.

300 B.C.
The Maya adopt the idea of a society in which kings and nobles reign over common people.

100 B.C.
The fall of the Olmec civilization.

The Cities

The first significant Maya settlements date back to 10,000 B.C., in the El Mirador basin, north of Petén. Most Maya cities were built during the Classic Period.

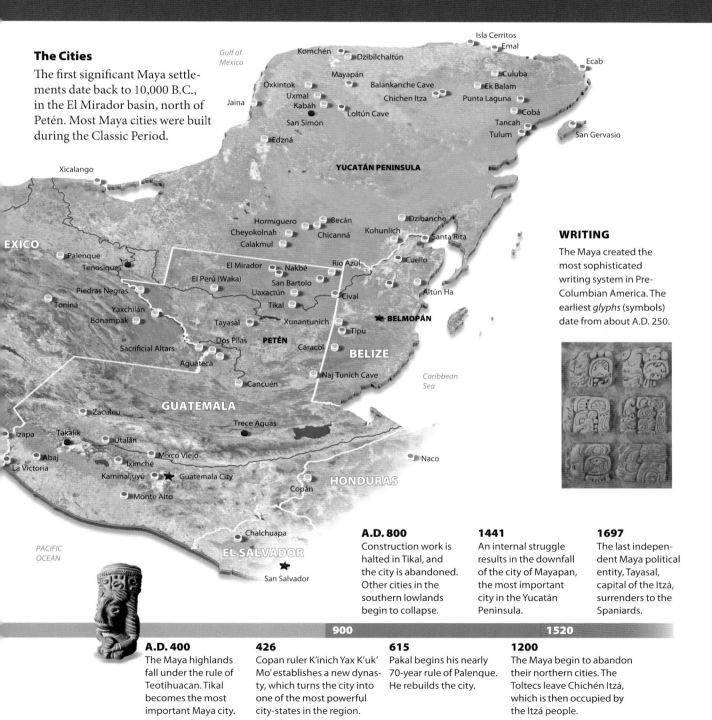

Gulf of Mexico

Komchén
Dzibilchaltún
Isla Cerritos
Emal
Ecab
Mayapán
Culuba
Oxkintok
Ek Balam
Balankanche Cave
Uxmal
Chichen Itza
Punta Laguna
Kabáh
Cobá
Loltún Cave
San Simón
Tancah
Jaina
Edzná
Tulum
San Gervasio

YUCATÁN PENINSULA

Xicalango

EXICO

Palenque
Tenosique
Piedras Negras
Toniná
Yaxchilán
Bonampak
Sacrificial Altars
Aguateca

Hormiguero
Becán
Dzibanche
Cheyokolnah
Chicanná
Kohunlich
Santa Rita
Calakmul
Cuello
El Mirador
Nakbé
Río Azul
El Perú (Waka)
San Bartolo
Uaxactún
Cival
Altún Ha
Tikal
★ **BELMOPÁN**
Tayasal
Xunantunich
Dos Pilas
Tipu
PETÉN
Caracol
BELIZE
Cancuén
Naj Tunich Cave

Caribbean Sea

Zaculeu
Trece Aguas
GUATEMALA
Izapa
Takalik
Utalán
Abaj
Mixco Viejo
Naco
La Victoria
Iximché
Kaminaljuyú ★ Guatemala City
HONDURAS
Monte Alto
Copán

PACIFIC OCEAN

Chalchuapa
EL SALVADOR
San Salvador

WRITING

The Maya created the most sophisticated writing system in Pre-Columbian America. The earliest *glyphs* (symbols) date from about A.D. 250.

A.D. 800
Construction work is halted in Tikal, and the city is abandoned. Other cities in the southern lowlands begin to collapse.

1441
An internal struggle results in the downfall of the city of Mayapan, the most important city in the Yucatán Peninsula.

1697
The last independent Maya political entity, Tayasal, capital of the Itzá, surrenders to the Spaniards.

900

1520

A.D. 400
The Maya highlands fall under the rule of Teotihuacan. Tikal becomes the most important Maya city.

426
Copan ruler K'inich Yax K'uk' Mo' establishes a new dynasty, which turns the city into one of the most powerful city-states in the region.

615
Pakal begins his nearly 70-year rule of Palenque. He rebuilds the city.

1200
The Maya begin to abandon their northern cities. The Toltecs leave Chichén Itzá, which is then occupied by the Itzá people.

Where Did the Maya Come From?

The heartland of the ancient Maya world lay in what is now the Petén region of modern-day Guatemala.

The Maya were one of many groups of Indians who have inhabited Mesoamerica—a region that includes what are now Mexico, Guatemala, and Honduras. People have lived in this region for at least 11,000 years.

The earliest inhabitants of Mesoamerica were hunters and gatherers. They got all their food from the plants and animals that grew naturally in their environment.

SETTLING EL PETÉN

Perhaps as early as 2000 B.C., the ancestors of the ancient Maya began to move into what is now the state of El Petén in Guatemala. Most scholars think these people came from coastal and highland regions along the Pacific coast. In the Petén lowlands, the people lived in small villages along rivers and lakes and hunted and gathered food in the nearby jungles. They also grew corn and other crops. In fact, they may have moved to the area seeking fertile land. By 800 B.C., the lowlands were completely settled.

THE OLMEC INFLUENCE

One of the first major centers of Middle American civilization was that of the Olmec Indians. They lived on the southern Gulf Coast in what are now the Mexican states of Veracruz and Tabasco. Between 1200 B.C. and 400 B.C., these Indians developed both a counting system and a calendar. They also had well-developed art.

Many scholars believe that the Olmec civilization greatly influenced Maya culture. Some scholars, however, think that the Maya developed independently. Still others argue that the Olmec and the earliest Maya were originally the same people.

THE CORN PEOPLE

The Maya themselves be–ieved they were descended from human beings created by the gods from yellow and white corn. The gods had first tried to create people from clay and then wood. But these early human forms were not able to worship the gods properly, and so the gods destroyed them.

The Wise Sons and Daughters of Corn

Corn was the main food of the ancient Maya. They grew many varieties of corn, including blue. Corn and its cultivation were cenral to the religious beliefs of the Maya people. They believed that the gods had made humans from corn. The Maya prayed to the corn god for plentiful harvests and offered sacrifices to him.

Maya women prepared corn in a variety of ways. They filled corn dough with meat, making what are today called tamales, and made corn flat bread, which today are called tortillas. The Maya also used corn to make an alcoholic drink called balche, which they sweetened with honey and spiced with bark.

OLMEC INFLUENCE

The Olmecs, whose huge carved stone heads are the most common symbol of their culture, greatly influenced Maya civilization. The heads weighed up to 36,000 pounds (16,300 kilograms) and stood over 9 feet (2.7 meters) high.

The Wonders of Chichén Itzá

Chichén Itzá was the most powerful Maya city between about A.D. 900 and 1200. Chichén's power was based on its military strength and its control over important trade routes that linked the Yucatán with central Mexico. As many as 50,000 people may have lived in the city and surrounding areas.

Central Chichén Itzá

included an immense plaza, the largest ball court in Mesoamerica, an astronomical observatory, *cenotes* (sinkholes), and the Kukulkán Pyramid.

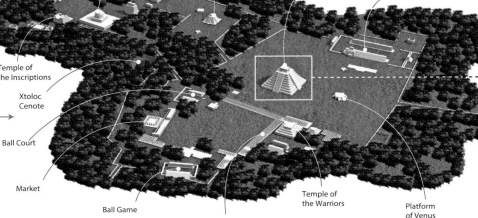

The Cloister
El Caracol (Observatory)
Red House
El Osario (Temple of the High Priest)
El Castillo (Kukulkán Pyramid)
The Great Ball Court
Temple of the Inscriptions
Xtoloc Cenote
Ball Court
Market
Ball Game
Group of a Thousand Columns
Temple of the Warriors
Platform of Venus

Kukulkán

Location:	20° 40' 01" N 88° 34' 09" W
Built:	A.D. 1000's
Orientation:	N +/- 20° toward geographical North.

Dimensions

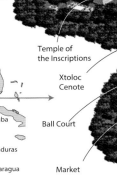

20 ft
78 ft
182 ft
182 ft

Marking the Year

Maya architects built many buildings to *align* (line up) with the movements of the sun and other celestial bodies.

Winter solstice
December 21 (day with the least hours of sunlight in the year)

Summer solstice
June 21 (day with the most hours of sunlight in the year)

Equinox
September 21 (day when the hours of sunlight are equal to those of darkness)

In mid-afternoon, light and shadow play on the north face to highlight the form of a snake descending the staircase.

SOUND OF THE QUETZAL

If a person stands facing the north stairs and claps, the resulting echo sounds like the chirp of the quetzal bird. For the Maya, the bird was a symbol of the creative force of life.

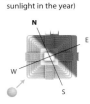

THE TEMPLE

A temple for religious ceremonies sits atop the pyramid. Here, Maya priests made animal and human sacrifices to Kukulkán.

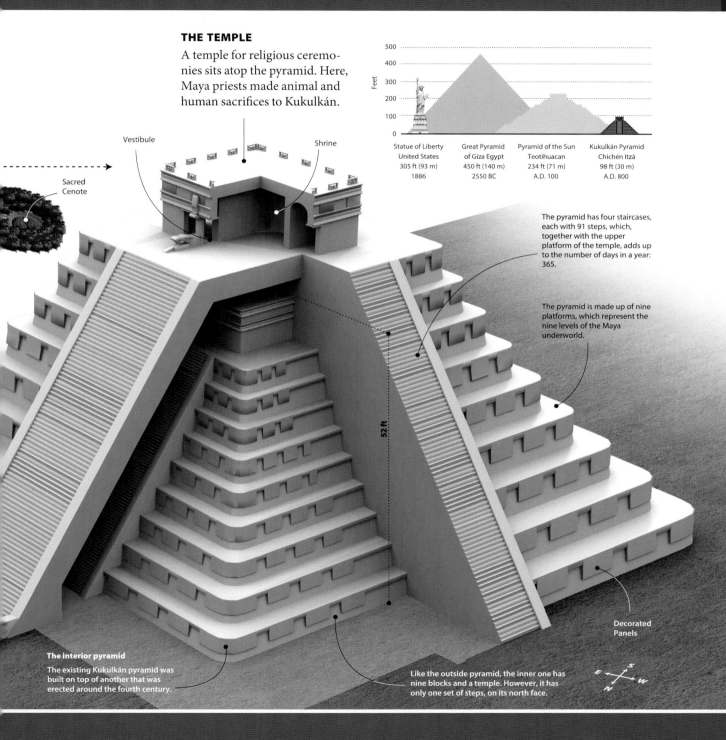

Vestibule

Shrine

Sacred Cenote

Statue of Liberty	Great Pyramid	Pyramid of the Sun	Kukulkán Pyramid
United States	of Giza Egypt	Teotihuacan	Chichén Itzá
305 ft (93 m)	450 ft (140 m)	234 ft (71 m)	98 ft (30 m)
1886	2550 BC	A.D. 100	A.D. 800

Feet
500
400
300
200
100
0

The pyramid has four staircases, each with 91 steps, which, together with the upper platform of the temple, adds up to the number of days in a year: 365.

The pyramid is made up of nine platforms, which represent the nine levels of the Maya underworld.

52 ft

Decorated Panels

The interior pyramid

The existing Kukulkán pyramid was built on top of another that was erected around the fourth century.

Like the outside pyramid, the inner one has nine blocks and a temple. However, it has only one set of steps, on its north face.

E · S · W · N

The Bonampak Murals

In the ruins of the city of Bonampak is a temple now known as the Temple of the Murals for the magnificent murals covering the walls of three rooms. The paintings, which were known only to local people until 1946, reveal the exquisite artistic achievements of the Maya people. Created in about A.D. 800, the murals are believed to depict life in the court of Chan Muán, the ruler of Bonampak.

FESTIVE OCCASION

Murals in the first room depict what may be the public presentation of a ... plays drums made from tortoise shells. Behind them two servants ...

CENTRAL FIGURE

A drummer with a feathered headdress separates two groups of percussion ...

A Fortunate Accident

The paintings of Bonampak were preserved by rain water. Leaks in the Temple of the Murals allowed rain to drip down the walls. Over time, a somewhat see-though layer of minerals was deposited on the walls. The mineral layer protected the paintings.

3 **THE MUSICIANS' MARCH**
Another group of musicians, dressed in festively colored robes, play

Other panels in the room illustrate trumpeters with wooden instruments.

Mysterious Maya Writing

The Maya are the only ancient American people known to have developed a writing system that could express all the words in their language. Their writing was a form of *hieroglyphics* (picture symbols).

After the Spaniards conquered the Maya, Maya scribes were forbidden to use their traditional writing. The Spaniards thought the writing was the work of the devil. They forced the Maya to write using the alphabet that Spaniards used to write their language—the same alphabet used to write English, French, and many other languages. As a result, the Maya lost the ability to read their own writing.

Modern scholars found Maya writing difficult to decipher, in part because they had no key. A key is a text with a message in both a known and unknown language. In addition, Maya writing is complex. Maya hieroglyphs, or glyphs, consist of a combination of ideograms, which represented entire ideas or words, and phonetic hieroglyphs, which represented syllables. In addition, syllables can usually be written in more than one way.

J. L. Stephens
(1805-1852)

The son of a businessman, John Lloyd Stephens was born in New Jersey. He studied law at Columbia University and worked as a lawyer in New York. he began to travel to exotic countries to improve his health. In 1839, U.S. President Martin Van Buren sent Stephens to Central America as an ambassador. His explorations of unknown Maya ruins in the region and his immensely popular books triggered new scientific and popular interest in the ancient Maya culture. Accompanied by the architect and illustrator Frederick Catherwood, he uncovered important archaeological sites, including Palenque, Uxmal, and Copán.

Alfred P. Maudslay
(1850-1931)

A British explorer and archaeologist, Maudslay was the first person to excavate ancient Maya sites. He was inspired by a lecture about the works of John Lloyd Stephens. He used scientifically exact methods in his excavations, which would later be copied by others who continued his work. Maudslay took the first archaeological surveys of Copán and Tikal, made careful plaster and papier-mâché casts of reliefs and sculptures, took photo-graphs, and made drawings that later had great historic value. He also explored Palenque and Chichén Itzá and became the first researcher to study Yaxchillan, a powerful city in the Postclassic Period, in modern-day Chiapas, Mexico. In 1902, Maudslay published the results of his research in the five-volume work *Biologia Centrali-Americana*.

Tatiana Proskouriakoff
(1905-1995)

Proskouriakoff, who was born in Russia and brought to the United States as a child, discovered that Maya glyphs recorded history. She took a job drawing reconstructions of ruins at Maya sites because she could not find architectural work, for which she was trained. She noticed a pattern to the *stelae* (commemorative stone slabs) set in front of temples. She saw that there was a stele for every five years of a king's reign. She then realized that the inscriptions on the stelae showed the dates of births, deaths, and other important events in the lives of kings and queens.

Yuri Valentinovich Knorozov
(1922-1999)

was a Russian language expert who challenged the widespread belief that each symbol in a Maya glyph stood for a whole word or idea. Knorosov discov-ered that Maya glyphs actually consisted of a combination of symbols. Some were *phonetic* (sound) symbols that stood for syllables, while others were *ideograms* (pictures) that stood for entire ideas or words.

Linda Schele
(1942-1998)

An American archaeologist and expert in Maya art and writing, Schele played an important role in deciphering Maya hieroglyphs. She left an enormous archive of photographs and drawings of Maya artistic works.

David Stuart
(1965-   )

The son of archaeologists studying the Maya, Stuart began working to decipher Maya glyphs when he was a teenager. He discovered that individual Maya words could be written using symbols that looked different but sounded the same (such as see and sea in English). In 1987, he published *Ten Phonetic Syllables*, which outlined a method for analyzing Maya writing that is widely used today. Stuart's method allowed Maya scholars to decipher many puzzling texts.

Sacred Ball Game

The Maya often played games to honor their gods. The most sacred of these was the ball game. Stone ball courts were a major feature of Maya capital cities.

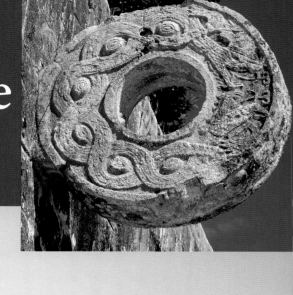

Playing to Honor the Gods

Religion played a central role in the life of the ancient Maya. They believed there was no real difference between sacred things and everyday things, including games. The ball game was the most sacred game. The Maya played many different versions of the ball game. In general, however, the object of the game was to move a rubber ball, probably from one end of a court to the other without using the hands.

Maya capital cities all had stone ball courts. The design of the courts changed over time. During the Classic Period, ball courts had sloping sides. In later times, the walls were vertical. High on each side at center court were stone rings, or some–times carved stone markers. Players tried to put the ball through the ring or hit the marker with the ball. The rubber ball was heavy, and players wore padding to protect their bodies from blows. Most Maya ball courts did not have seats for spectators, though some had steps that could have seated several thousand people. The largest Maya ball court is found in the Post-classic city of Chichén Itzá. It is about the size of an American football field (120 yards [110 meters] in length).

Sometimes, players were sacrificed after a game. Scholars once believed that the losing captain or team was sacrificed. Now, some think it was the winning captain or team who were killed. The winners would have been seen as a worthy sacrifice to the gods. During the Post-classic Period, sacrificial victims were sometimes tied up tightly and used as a ball during a ball game.

BALL COURT AT UXMAL

The ball court at Chichén Itzá (above), with its vertical walls, is typical of the playing fields built during the Postclassic Period. Players tried to put a ball through the stone rings (inset) that sat high on the walls—without using their hands.

Blood Sacrifice

The Maya believed that a sacred energy, or life force, ran through everything in the universe. This life force, called k'uh *(k OOH)* was closely related to blood. For this reason, blood was sacred. The blood sacrifice of ball players and other human victims was one way in which the Maya honored their gods. Blood and human sacri–fice, which were linked to ideas of death and rebirth, were major elements in the Maya story explaining the origin of the universe.

Deer, dogs, and turkeys were sacrificed to feed the gods. During religious ceremonies, Mayan kings, queens, and priests, as well as ordinary people, fre-quently offered their own blood, which they spattered on pieces of bark paper. They pierced their tongues, cheeks, and other body parts with sharp shells, stingray spines, and razor-sharp blades carved from obsidian. The pain and blood loss they experienced, combined with the use of mind-altering drugs, caused them to have visions. The Maya believed these visions were messages from the gods.

Mysteries of Maya Science and Mathematics

The ancient Maya were gifted mathematicians and astronomers whose calendars guided nearly all aspects of their life.

Precise, remarkably accurate calendars are among the greatest achievements of the ancient Maya civilization. Carefully marking the passage of time was an essential part of daily Maya life. As an agricultural people, the Maya needed to track the changing seasons to know when to plant their crops. But Maya calendars mainly served a sacred purpose—recording the religious ceremonies that lay at the center of their lives. Each day, called a k'in *(k EEN),* had its own importance, and many days were celebrated with festivals and sacrifices. The most important of these events marked the ends of such Maya time cycles as months, years, and longer periods made up of many years. The Maya believed that these ceremonies pleased the gods, who then kept the Maya well fed, healthy, and safe from harm. The Maya also believed that the movements of the stars and planets could be used to explain the past and predict the future.

OBSERVING THE SKY

The Maya created their calendars using advanced mathematics and a detailed knowledge of the movements of the sun, moon, stars, and planets. The Maya were expert astronomical observers who made their calculations without telescopes or other instruments. Mayan architects built many buildings to *align* (line up) with astronomical events. In some cities, observatories sat atop temples. Inside these chambers, Maya priests placed two crossed pieces of wood, providing a fixed point for observing the sky. Many sites have a group of buildings or hilltops that align with important positions of the sun, such as sunrise on the day on which a season begins or sunset on another day with astronomical significance.

MAYA CALENDARS

The Maya developed a number of calendars. One of these calendars, called the Tzolk'in *(tzohl KEEN),* was an *almanac* (calendar of important events) of 260 days. Each day in the Tzolk'in was named with 1 of 20 day names and was given a number from 1 to 13. Each of the 20 day names had a god or goddess associated with it. Maya priests predicted good or bad luck by studying the combination of gods or goddesses and numbers. Children were named according to the day on which they were born.

The Maya also had a calendar of 365 days called the Haab (hahb). This calendar

Observing the Sky

Like many other ancient peoples, the Maya found familiar shapes in the arrangement of stars in the night sky. The Pleiades star cluster was seen as a form with rattles taken from a rattlesnake. Gemini was considered to be a turtle. The North Star commanded the Maya's attention because it seemed to remain in the same place in the sky all night. They associated the North Star with Xaman Ek, the monkey-faced god of travelers.

EL CARACOL
observatory in Chichén Itzá has a functional and characteristic round design.

Records in Stone

The Maya developed the only complete writing system in ancient America. This means they could graphically represent spoken speech in its entirety. In addition to narrating the history of their kings, much of Maya writing—in books, the stelae, and reliefs—records astronomical events. This became very useful in the early days of deciphering the Maya writing system, in the late 1800's and early 1900's. In 1906, the German historian Ernst Förstemann discovered many numerical coincidences related to the planet Venus in Maya book known as the Dresden Codex. These early studies made it possible to recognize the advanced knowledge in astronomy that was achieved by the Maya.

was based on the solar year (the orbit of Earth around the sun). This calendar divided the year into 18 months of 20 days each, plus 5 days at the end of the year called the wayeb *(wah YAHB)*. To the Maya, the wayeb was extrem–ely unlucky. During this period, they made many sacrifices, went without food, and avoided unnecessary work.

The Maya combined the Tzolk'in and Haab to create the Round Calendar. A Calendar Round date consists of the Tzolk'in date and the Haab date.

The same combination of these specific dates repeats only once every 52 years.

THE LONG COUNT CALENDAR

The longest calendar of the Maya tracked a period of about 5,128 years. This Long Count Calendar measured time from the day on which the Maya believed the world was created. This date was August 13, 3114 B.C., by western calendars. Because Long Count dates did not repeat, this system was used on monuments to record important events.

Many scholars calculated that the Mayan Long Count cycle was scheduled to end on December 21, 2012, on the western calendar. Some people came to believe that the calendar forecast the end of all time. But archaeologists who study the ancient Maya noted that no predictions of the end of the world exist in Maya writings or inscriptions. They also pointed out that the end of the Long Count Calendar on December 21, 2012, simply marks the beginning of a new calendar cycle.

MAYA MATHEMATICS

The Maya used a mathematical system based on the number 20, instead of 10, as in the decimal system. A dot represented the number one; a bar represented five; and special symbols represented zero. The Maya were among the first people to use symbols for the idea of zero. It is still unclear whether the Maya were the inventors of the concept of zero, or if this knowledge was inherited from the Olmecs.

CREDIBLE CHRONICLE
The glyphs tell of the ascent to the throne of the son of King Pakal, K'inich K'an Joy Chitam II, shown at center flanked by his parents.

The Cycle of Venus

The Dresden Codex includes accurate, detailed information on the cycles of Venus. The appearance of the planet in the sky was often a signal for war. The Maya glyph for *war* is made up the sign for Venus and one other sign. That other sign is often the glyph for the city that was attacked in a war or battle. Scholars have found that 70 percent of the appearances of this "star war" sign happened at times when Venus was in the sky as the evening star.

The Mystery of "Maya Blue"

For the Maya, a brilliant blue pigment often used in murals and for pottery and other objects was valued for more than its beauty. The color, known today as Maya blue, played an important role in rituals and sacrifices. Some people marked for sacrifice may have been covered with the pigment before they were thrown into the cenotes. The pigment has proven remarkably durable against weather, acids, water, and even time.

How the Maya made the blue pigment has long puzzled scientists. In the 1960's, chemists discovered that Maya blue was a mixture mainly of indigo, a deep blue dye made from the indigo plant, and a kind of clay called palygorskite that was heated. But modern scientists are still trying to determine the exact "recipe" of the mixture and the process by which the pigment was made.

What Happened to the Maya Codices?

To the conquering Spaniards, the Maya's books were "astonishing." But they also believed these beautiful books were the work of the devil.

In 1545, a Spanish missionary named Diego de Landa arrived in Yucatán and began traveling from town to town to learn about the Maya. He learned their language and studied their customs. De Landa was permitted to see and touch treasured, handwritten books now known as codices (plural for *codex*). Made of tree-bark paper, the codices consisted of long strips folded together. The strips were inscribed with hieroglyphic writing and drawings.

De Landa and his fellow missionaries spent a number of years unsuccessfully trying to convert the Maya to Christianity. Finally, de Landa turned to violence. He tortured and executed Maya who refused to abandon their traditional religion. He demolished Maya temples, though he was entranced by their "astonishing height and beauty." He wrote of the Maya calendar, "Whoever ordered the counting of the days, if it was the devil, did so for his honor; if it was a man, he must have been very *idolatrous* [worshiping idols]."

BOOK BURNING

De Landa also burned hundreds of Maya codices. He said, "We found a large number of these books ... and because there was nothing that didn't have superstition and lies of the devil, we burned them all, which amazed and saddened them."

De Landa's campaign against the Maya came to the attention of the Spanish king, who forced him to return to Spain to account for his actions. While in Spain, de Landa wrote *Relación de las cosas de Yucatán (Concerning Things of the Yucatán)*. The book included a brief description of the Maya calendar and a *phonetic transcription* (representation of sounds) of the text in Span-ish. Ironically, the book is now one of the most important sources of information about the Maya, a culture that the author had tried to crush. In 1573, de Landa returned to Yucatán, only to die six years later.

SURVIVORS

Only three codices known to be authentic exist in a state that allows them to be handled or read. They are the *Dresden Codex,* a book about astronomy, kept in Vienna, Austria; the *Tro-Cortesianus Codex,* a book of predictions, kept in Madrid; and the *Paris Codex,* a book describing rituals, kept in Paris.

Scholars disagree whether a fourth codex, called the *Grolier Codex,* is real. It was discovered in Chiapas state in modern-day Mexico in 1965. The codice is named for a club in New York City where it was displayed. The *Grolier Codex* is kept in Mexico City.

MEMOIR

A scene from the *Tro-Cortesianus Codex*, kept in Madrid, Spain, shows a pair of gods associated with 1 of the 260 days in the sacred Maya *Tzolk'in* calendar.

The *Books of Chilam Balam*

After the devastating loss of their codices, the Maya began to record their history in the *Books of Chilam Balam (Books of the Jaguar Shaman)*. However, the Spaniards forbade Maya scribes to use their traditional writing. Instead, the scribes were forced to use the alphabet used to write Spanish. This alphabet, known as the Roman alphabet, is also used to write English. Spanish priests taught the Maya to use the Roman alphabet.

The *Chilam Balam* were named for the towns where they were made. Among the most important are the *Chilam Balam* of Mani, Tizimin, Chumayel, Kaua, Ixil, and Tusik.

The *Chilam Balam* are especially interesting to scholars because some of the books record events from the little-known Postclassic Period. Some of the books are copies of codices that were destroyed by the Spaniards.

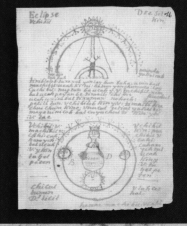

Maya Treasures

The Maya were exceptional artists who produced paintings, sculptures, and carvings of great beauty, often in vivid colors. They were also master stone carvers who created their masterpieces using stone tools, because they had no metal tools. Jade, which symbolized life, was the most appreciated and sought-after stone.

Mask of Pakal

The splendid funerary mask of King K'inich Janaab' Pakal of Palenque, located in what is now Chiapas state in Mexico, dates from the A.D. 600's. It consists of 340 pieces of carefully assembled jade. The jade pieces in the mask are from 0.08 to 2.76 inches (2 to 7 centimeters) long. The eyes are made of pearl and obsidian.

Pakal is the only Meso–american ruler whose tomb—discovered in 1952—was found inside a pyramid (the Temple of the Inscriptions). Remarkably, the tomb had not been looted.

Pakal was a prosperous king who commissioned numerous buildings and monuments during his long reign of 68 years. He is well-known because the cover of his *sarcophagus* (stone coffin) depicts him in a pose that some have associated with that of a modern astronaut. In fact, he is shown falling into the underworld.

"DAZZLING" URN
The beauty of this vase resulted in its nickname, "the dazzler." It was found in the Margarita Tomb at Copán (Honduras). It belonged to the wife of a king of the city. Found with the urn were other vessels that held offerings for the afterlife.

JADE ORNAMENT
A delicate jade chest piece shows the image of a god, flanked at the top by two heads. It dates from the Classic Period.

VASE
The image of a priest richly dressed in a patterned robe and an feathered headdress decorates a cylindrical vessel found at Tikal (Guatemala).

Rulers of the Land

A lavish headdress and elaborate clothing mark a seated figure as a member of the Maya elite. The amazing level of detail in this and similiar figurines from the Classic Period has led some archaeologists to suggest that such terra-cotta statues may represent actual historical people.

STELA

King Uaxaklajuun Ub'aah K'awiil, also known as 18 Rabbit, is represented in a stela from Copán. The Maya created many of these tall, elaborately carved monuments. They usually portray kings or rulers and almost always include glyphs with historical data. Stelae have been a valuable source of information about the ancient Maya.

EAR JEWELRY

An ear flare from the early Classic Period is made of shell and decorated with the profile of a ruler. Commonly worn by Maya elites, these disks were thought to have been attached to a weighted cord that was passed through the ear lobe.

ECCENTRICS

Strange figures, called eccentrics, were chipped from flint (above) or *obsidian* (volcanic rock). Human profiles were carved along the edges with remarkable skill.

The Splendor of Copán

Copán, one of the most prosperous and powerful Maya cities of the Classical Period, was a populous metropolis at its peak. Its artistic treasures are among the most beautiful and outstanding of all ancient Maya art.

The King's Feast

Uaxaklajuun Ub'aah K'awiil (right), ruler of Copán from A.D. 695 to 738, watches a ball game with his family as servants offer him food and drink and shade him with a parasol. Uaxaklajuun Ub'aah K'awiil, named "18 Rabbit" by archaeologists, ruled over the city at the height of its splendor. He built numerous structures, including a building that symbolized the mountain from which, the Maya believed, their ancestors first obtained corn seeds. Among Uaxaklajuun Ub'aah K'awiil's many monuments were numerous *stelae* (stone slabs) that depicted him as a god. The ball court he commissioned was finished in 738, shortly before he was overthrown and beheaded by a rebellious subject.

Who Was the "Red Queen"?

The remains of an elderly woman surrounded by many valuable objects were found in a tomb at Copán in 1993. The woman has become known as the "Red Queen" or "Lady in Red," because her bones were covered in red pigment. Some archaeologists believe she was the wife of the founder of the Copán dynasty.

ABSOLUTE RULER
Uaxaklajuun Ub'aah K'awiil was the 13th successor of the king who founded Copán in A.D. 426. The dynasty ruled the city for almost 400 years.

What Caused the Decline of Maya Cities?

For many years, scholars attributed the decline of the Maya civilization to natural disasters or deadly epidemics. Today, most researchers lean toward a combination of factors: drought, overpopulation, depletion of resources, and war.

Beginning in about A.D. 750, at the height of their civilization, the Maya stopped constructing temples and other major buildings, carving monuments, and erecting stelae in their lowland cities. The population of these cities dropped significantly, and one by one, they were abandoned. Scholars are still trying to discover the reasons for the collapse of Classic Maya society in the lowlands.

DAMAGING DROUGHTS

Some experts blame a series of serious droughts. They think the ancient Maya fled their cities for more favorable farming regions in the highlands of Chiapas and in the Yucatán region in modern-day Mexico. In fact, as cities in the lowlands were abandoned, cities in northern areas rose to great power.

A PLAGUE OF PROBLEMS

Other scholars think that drought was just one of many factors that caused the Classic-Period collapse. By this time, many lowland city-states had large populations. For centuries, the Maya had been able to produce abundant food without seriously damaging the relatively poor soils of the rain forest. As droughts attacked the land, the Maya began to clear more of the rain forest for farming and to increase their use of irrigation, which produced more erosion. These farming methods exhausted the land and caused crop failures. Famine and disease may have followed.

Archaeologists have found evidence that fighting among city-states became more common toward the end of the Classic Period. For centuries, the Maya city-states, for the most part, had been able to live together peacefully. They fought against each other in small wars from time to time. Afterward, the ruler of the conquered city was usually sacrificed. But the city-states generally shared culture, traded, and did not destroy defeated cities.

At the end of the Classic Period, this changed. Some experts believe scarce water and food forced Maya city-states to compete for natural resources. Populations began to shrink as death rates rose and birth rates fell.

FINAL CHAPTER

Archaeologists have found that no major buildings were constructed after 830. The last known carving from the heart of the Classic Maya civilization was dated January 15, 910. This magnificent period in Maya history had ended.

Massacre at Cancuén

Skeletons of murdered nobles found in the ruins of Cancuén provide chilling evidence of the turmoil in the Maya lowlands at the end of the Classic Period. In November 2005, archaeologist Arthur Demarest discovered the bones of some 30 members of Cancuén's elite in a sacred reservoir. The finely adorned victims, who included men, women, and children, had been murdered by lance thrusts to the head or neck. Many of the bodies had been dismembered. Nearby were the graves of the king and queen of the city, who had also been executed. The skeletons of another dozen slaughtered nobles were found in a third grave. Archaeologists are unsure whether the attackers were from Cancuén itself or another city-state. After the massacre, Cancuén, one of the wealthiest Maya cities of that period, was abandoned.

Doorways to the Underworld

For the Maya, deep wells called cenotes represented sacred openings to the underworld inhabited by the rain god Chac. Underwater archaeologists have retrieved many objects, including human bones, weapons, tools, and jewelry, that were thrown into the cenotes by the ancient Maya.

Preserving Artifacts

Human remains and other artifacts may be preserved underwater for hundreds of years. Cold temperatures, low oxygen levels in the water, and the formation of a covering from sand, shells, or other natural materials can protect these objects. When they are brought to the surface, however, oxygen in the air triggers chemical changes that cause them to decay rapidly. To prevent further deterioration, archaeologists first place artifacts in an environment similar to that in which they were found. Specialists called restorers then work to preserve the objects.

ROAD TO THE UNDERWORLD
To the Maya of Yucatán, the cenotes, such as the one in Chichén Itzá (above), were entrances to the afterlife.

Working Underwater

Like archaeologists working on land, underwater archaeologists describe, map, draw, and photograph sites and artifacts. They also use special techniques to uncover and retrieve objects.

RECORDING
Archaeologists use special pens and coated paper to take notes underwater.

LIFTING BALLOONS
Objects that are too large or heavy to be carried by the diver are sent to the surface by balloon.

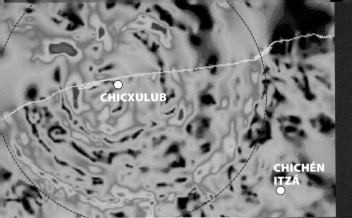

How Were Cenotes Created?

Cenotes are natural sinkholes formed where water has eroded away or dissolved rock. Many of the cenotes on the Yucatán Peninsula can be found along the rim of the Chicxulub Crater. This ancient crater, which is about 110 miles (177 kilometers) in diameter, was created about 65 million years ago when a huge asteroid crashed into Earth. The fires and dust clouds resulting from the impact are believed to have killed off the last of the dinosaurs.

Underwater Robot

Small, remotely operated underwater vehicles (ROV's) are used to reach places that are too small, deep, or dangerous for divers to go. These robotic devices are equipped with lamps and video cameras. Some ROV's also have sensors for record–ing water conditions and mechanical arms for grasping objects.

ADDITIONAL SENSORS
PROPULSORS
LIGHT
21 IN
CAMERA

GRID

A portable grid can be used for mapping a site and to hold objects in place so they can be drawn or photographed.

AIRLIFT

To "dig" underwater, archaeolo-gists often use a device called an airlift. Compressed air is pumped into the tube to create suction. The action pulls sediment and small objects to a mesh cage at the surface for examination.

Places to See and Visit

OTHER PLACES OF INTEREST

COPÁN
HONDURAS

The city reached its zenith during the Classic Period. Its art was highly sophisticated. The main structures include the Temple of Rosalila, the Q Altar, and numerous pillars, many of which represent kings. Copán has been a United Nations (UN) World Heritage Site since 1980.

CANCUÉN
GUATEMALA

Although this city in the Petén region is less important than Tikal or Calakmul, it contains one of the largest Maya palaces. In 2005, a series of royal tombs linked to the fall of the Maya civilization was discovered here.

CALAKMUL
MEXICO

Located in the Petén region of Mexico, Calakmul is one of the largest Maya archaeological sites. Calakmul rivaled Tikal during the Classic Period. Its pyramids are among the highest built by the Maya.

BONAMPAK
MEXICO

In the Maya language, its name means *painted walls*. The city has many splendid murals, painted in vivid colors. A reproduction of the murals hangs in the National Museum of Anthropology in Mexico City.

EL MIRADOR
GUATEMALA

A large archaeological site in the Petén region, El Mirador includes some of the tallest building complexes of the Maya culture, including El Tigre and La Danta pyramids. The city stands out from other Maya centers because its enormous pyramids date from the Preclassic Period.

UXMAL
MEXICO

Located on the Yucatán Peninsula, Uxmal flourished during the Postclassic Period. The city's Pyramid of the Magician is the only Maya building with rounded sides. The ruins have been a UN World Heritage Site since 1996.

Chichén Itzá, Tourist Epicenter

THE CASTLE

Located on the Yucatán Peninsula in modern-day Mexico, Chichén Itzá is one of the best known cities of the ancient Maya and one of the most visited locations in all of the Americas. Its age of splendor dates to the Postclassic Period. It has characteristics that reflect Toltec influence. A pyramid known as "El Castillo" (the Castle or Kukulkán's Pyramid) is the city's most notable building. Chichén Itzá's sacred cenote is one of the most explored by archaeologists.

ACCESS AND ATTRACTIONS

Tourists generally arrive at Chichén Itzá by airplane or bus from the beaches of Cancún or Cozumel. Both of these resort towns have their own Maya ruins. In addition to archaeological tourism, the Yucatán Peninsula is famous for its varied and interesting plant and animal life. Touring the ruins of Chichén Itzá takes about three hours.

RECOMMENDATIONS

Chichén Itzá is the second-most important archaeological tourism site in Mexico. It is located in the state of Yucatán and is 75 miles (120 kilometers) from its capital, Merida. The climate is warm, and it generally rains in the summer. During the equinoxes (particularly on the spring equinox), Chichén Itzá is crowded with tourists wanting to see the "descent of the serpent" on Kukulkán's Pyramid. The pyramid has been closed to climbing since 2006.

Grand Tikal

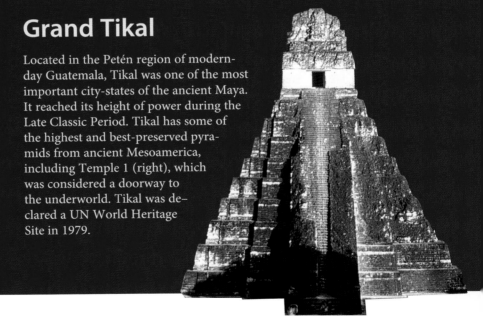

Located in the Petén region of modern-day Guatemala, Tikal was one of the most important city-states of the ancient Maya. It reached its height of power during the Late Classic Period. Tikal has some of the highest and best-preserved pyramids from ancient Mesoamerica, including Temple 1 (right), which was considered a doorway to the underworld. Tikal was declared a UN World Heritage Site in 1979.

MAYAPAN
MEXICO

Founded during the Postclassic Period near Chichén Itzá, Mayapan was the most powerful city in Yucatán until just before the arrival of the Spaniards in the Americas. The main buildings are very similar to those at Chichén Itzá.

PALENQUE
MEXICO

Located in the state of Chiapas, this Classic-Period city is small compared with Tikal. Its fame is due mainly to the tomb of King Pakal, found in the Temple of the Inscriptions. A UN World Heritage Site since 1987, Palenque is one of the most studied archaeological sites.

Glossary

Archaeologist – A scientist who studies the remains of past human cultures.

Astronomy – The study of the universe and the objects in it.

Bloodletting – Drawing blood from the fingertips, earlobes, or other parts of the body with a sharp object as part of a religious ritual.

Cenotes – Natural sinkholes or pits in the ground formed where water has eroded away or dissolved rock.

City-state – An independent state consisting of a city and the territories dependent on it.

Civilization – The way of life in a society that features complex economic, governmental, and social systems.

Codex: – An early book (plural is codices).

Culture – A term used by social scientists for a way of life. Culture includes a society's arts, beliefs, customs, institutions, inventions, language, technology, and values.

Drought – A long period without rain.

Elite – A member of the upper class of a society.

Epigraphers – Scholars who study inscriptions.

Fertile – Able to produce crops (when used about land or soil).

Funerary mask – A mask placed on the face of a dead person during a burial; a cast of a person's face made after death.

Glyph – Hieroglyphs; a picture symbol in certain writing systems that could be used to stand for an idea, a sound, or a name.

Hunter-gatherer – A person who obtains food by hunting wild animals and gathering plants.

Ideogram – Pictures that stand for ideas or words.

Inscription – Words or symbols written, carved, or engraved on a monument, sculpture, piece of pottery, or other object.

Jade – A hard, tough, and highly colored stone that comes in a range of colors.

K'in (k EEN) – A day on the Maya calendar.

K'uh (k OOH) – A sacred energy or life force closely related to blood that the Maya believed ran through everything in the universe.

Mesoamerica – The area that covers what are now Mexico and Central America.

Monumental buildings – Large, important buildings such as temples, palaces, or tombs.

Mural – A painting on the walls or ceiling of a building.

Myth – A story told to explain the world and its mysteries.

Natural resources – Materials in or around Earth that are important or even necessary for life, including air, sunshine, water, metals, and oil.

Obsidian – A natural glass formed when hot lava flows onto the surface of Earth and cools.

Palanquin – A framework to be carried on men's shoulders or by beasts of burden, with a couch usually enclosed by curtains.

Peasant – Any farm laborer of low social status.

Phonetic: – Having to do with the sound or a syllable or word.

Pyramid – A large building or other structure with a square base and four smooth, triangular-shaped sides that come to a point at the top, or, in Mesoamerica and South America, that are flat at the top.

Rain forest – An area of tall trees growing in a region of year-round warmth and abundant rainfall, usually found at or near the equator.

Reservoir – A place where water is collected and stored for use.

Ritual – A solemn or important act or ceremony, often religious is nature.

Social class – A group of people who share a common status or position in society. Social classes represent differences in wealth, power, employment, family background, or other qualities.

Society – People living together as a group.

Slash and burn agriculture – A system in which vegetation is burned and used as fertilizer for land with poor soil.

Solar cycle – A year; the amount of time it takes Earth to circle the sun.

Stela – An upright slab or pillar of stone carved with an inscription or sculptured design describing gods as well as rulers and events from Maya history (plural is stelae).

Terrace – A flat, raised piece of land used for growing crops that is built on a mountain slope and surrounded by a small wall.

For Further Information

Books

Bell-Rehwoldt, Sheri. *Maya: Amazing Inventions You Can Build Yourself.* White River Junction, VT: Nomad, 2012. Print.

Currie, Stephen. *Mayan Mythology.* Detroit, MI: Lucent, 2012. Print.

Harris, Nathaniel, and Elizabeth Graham. *Ancient Maya: Archaeology Unlocks the Secrets to the Maya's Past.* Washington, DC: National Geographic, 2008. Print.

Pipe, Jim. *Mysteries of the Mayan Calendar.* New York: Crabtree, 2013. Print.

Schomp, Virginia. *The Ancient Maya.* New York: Marshall Cavendish Benchmark, 2010. Print.

Websites

Cecil, Jessica. "The Fall of the Mayan Civilisation." *BBC History.* BBC, 17 Feb. 2011. Web. 07 Feb. 2014.

"Collapse: Why Do Civilizations Fail?" *Annenberg Learner.* Annenberg Foundation, 2014. Web. 07 Feb. 2014.

"Maya." *The British Museum.* Trustees of the British Museum, n.d. Web. 07 Feb. 2014.

"The Maya." *Living Maya Time.* Smithsonian Institution, 2014. Web. 07 Feb. 2014.

"Pre-Hispanic City of Chichen-Itza." *UNESCO World Heritage Centre.* UNESCO World Heritage Centre, 2014. Web. 07 Feb. 2014.

Index

Acknowledgments